Piece of Poetry

Me and Me

RAVIRAJ MISHRA

Raviraj Mishra

www.ravirajmishra.com

www.instagram.com/imravirajmishra/

Cover design by Raviraj Mishra

Book Edited by Ruchira Tilekar

DEDICATED TO

Kedarnath Mishra

Mamata Mishra

Rajani Mishra

ABOUT PIECE OF POETRY

We were introduced to poetry right from a young age. We were made to sing and recite poetry in groups. The rhyming words somehow would bring a sense of enjoyment, and they won't leave our mind even with the passing days. Poetry holds magic. A magic to change the moment and bring out the joyous hidden self. We all in some point or another had come across a poetry that either taught us the unlearned or brought back a memory or just a smile.

Piece of poetry *is an effort to share my thoughts through prose. Each poetry was written with a story in mind, willing to be talked about. The thoughts that didn't need sophisticated words, but they were craving for rhythm.*

The idea was to point out some of the feelings and emotions that were desperate to be shared. Some untold words, a certain perspective that was always doubted by self and others. ***Piece of poetry*** *is an honest attempt to format these feelings into a song, hoping that it would stick with everyone who decided to read it.*

I hope you all enjoy and feel the depth of each word.

ME and ME

We search the whole world for all our necessities, the necessity of love, the necessity of care and, etc. However, we forget to appreciate and understand ourselves.

The importance of our own self is somewhere lost in between favouring the world. But if we don't know who we really are! we can't appreciate the real world. Let alone loving it.

ME and ME, *is an idea to talk about our own self.*

*The importance of self-love, self-care, and self-talk is been shared under the umbrella of **Me and ME.***

Raviraj Mishra

CONTENTS

Poetry is the spontaneous overflow of powerful feelings: it takes its origin from emotion recollected in tranquillity.

William Wordsworth

IT NEEDS A BLOW!

Vigilante enough,
not to fall.
Dry like summer,
I hated it all.

The idea of rain
gave me hope.
Haunted I was,
what if it stalled!
Unjust behavior
towards self.
Dreading, dwelling
in particular hell.

Escape sequences
ran through my head,
it was night
with screening noir.
The survival instincts
accelerated hope.

What silence couldn't give,
was given to me
by my words.

Wrote and wrote from evening to dawn.

Got myself an idea
to make it heard.
Trapped in reality for many,
a dying fire
beneath our ribs.

Cursing, unsetting,
installing pain.
Trust me,
it just needs a blow!

REALIZATION

Eyes sore.
Heart breaks.
Pathetic thoughts.
Seldom true.

Assuming mind.
Challenging questions.
Bad reasons.
Thought of two,
but nothing new.

Just same old mess
of cursing love,
Attached to people.
Forgetting real purpose.

Self-talks came natural.
Finding meaning,
if there's any!
Perpetual lessons.
Until realization.

I SAW A KNIGHT

I closed my eyes and
saw a knight.

His face was covered
in dark and trouble.

His posture straight
hinting that he belonged.
He belonged to a normal tribe,
with people of normal thoughts
and normal life.

Interesting was
what he wanted to find,
it had an essence of
freedom, hope, and dream.

He worked for the king
and his kingdom.
They paid him handful
and always told him –
his service was needed.

He loved his kingdom

but there was not a war to fight.
Just some
daily tantrums
of the kings' subjects
and some rules
he had to make sure
that everyone will abide.

His mind was
somewhere else,
where there was
light and snow.
The mountain ranges,
where there was
no king or his foe.

He no longer wanted to be a knight,
a shining armor for him
was cheaper than the dream of his life.

Enough time
he had wasted already,
leaving the comfort
was only his choice.

I closed my eyes and
saw a knight.

The knight was no one else
but me,
the structured world was
paying me handful,
to live a life,
they had designed.

The comfort they provided
was non resistible,
but it killed passion and
spark that was irreplaceable.

Surely many of us would feel
that it was the way of life,
getting a job,
working day and night,
for an amount
to spend on liabilities
and in the end
restraining ourselves
from overusing it.

Just like the knight,
I too had lost the love
for this shining armor of mine.

The rules and patterns

had nothing to do with
what I had defined
for my life.

Enough time
I had wasted already,
leaving the comfort
was my only choice.

BROKEN STARS

Who searches
for the broken stars?
For those who are interested
shall look at it
with greedy heart.

Assuming that
the one who is broken
might care for the world
and it's wishes
for the diamonds and pearl.

But the broken ones
always curse!
They curse for their pain,
they curse for there
is nothing broken
but them.

Who searches for the broken stars?
There are some
who look at it
with pain in their heart.

Relating to its pain,
the fall, the fear and
the loss of hope.

They curse the destiny
along with the broken stars.

IGNORE

I know it's my true inner self,
suggesting me to ignore.

Ignore the world
that teases you
when you are blind folded.

Ignore the ones
who express their disappointment,
when it's easier.

Ignore the missions
given to you
by people who want you to fail.

Ignore the existence of the ones
who think they can use you,
when it's convenient.

Ignore the possibilities of giving up,
for there are people,
who are still working for it.

Ignore the easiest ways,

for nothing worthy happens there.
Ignore the senses,
your mind,
and listen to what your heart says.

For intuitions are born there
and they somehow know
what you really want.

NO ONE CARES WHO I AM

For some I am a treasure,
while some blame me
for their pain.

Some complain about the way
I live while others
admire my life.

No one cares who I am,
everyone believes
what I present.

Now it's hard that
I will be different again.
So, stop wishing and
burn down your hopes.

My lies have taken over my life
and surprisingly
this is what
I live from now on.

I would make you laugh
just like the clowns do.

But do remember there
will always be a mask
that would cover
what I really own.

YOU THAT LIVES INSIDE

Bring me back
from the worse and
lift me up to the sky.

For all my hopes are on you.
You that lives inside.

The stronger,
wiser and the bold one.

Keep me steady and
force me to fly.
Until I touch the moon
and bring back
all that shines.

I haven't slept for nights,
go ahead and
sing me a sweet lullaby.

Don't hate my mess,
for it's us
who have to deal.

I can't regret it
no more.

If you think,
 it's not worth it.
Just walk with me
and listen, my life story
I will let you know.

IMPORTANT TO BREATH

I kept sleeping,
ignoring all the wounds I had.
It made my sleep worse
but waking up was more difficult.

The mysterious of my mind
continued to bully me.
My heart was its arena
to play all the levels of the game
of breaking me bad.

I couldn't rise,
let alone I would desire to fight.
I wished everything
remained black when I wake up.

Not a single emotion I wanted to see.
I knew I would get all pieces back
and fix them tighter
this time not to bleed.

I reached at the edge
of the morning.
I felt sober

and less pain.

My blood was back
on its track to the heart.
I was ready again to dance
to all the beats of
togetherness with someone.

But this time
living less on possibilities
and more by the importance
to breath.

CONCRETE

Do you ever wonder
why your heart is attached
to the concrete?
The city of lives
moving everywhere?

Why you love
the never-ending crowd?
The always shining days
whether its quarter past 3
in the morning with full moon
or no moon.

Have you ever
found yourself
looking at the ocean waves
trying to tickle the rocks
and the sands on its bay?

Why you love to rise
in a place you don't
know a bit about
but still love the

aroma around.

It's in the box of heart
where lies a dream
to move around,
be a victim of this
never-ending desire
to find a new place
and be a part of a
new crowd.

THE 'UNKNOWN' IN MY HOUSE

The 'unknown' in my house.
Disturbing the silence,
injecting madness,
twisting my morals,
reviewing every ounce of
sophistication in me,
only to reject it and
reconfigure the complete system.

The 'unknown' in my house.
Rational when decisive
and high when need to be sober.
Delusional when dreaming
and stubborn when establishing.

The 'unknown' in my house.
Caring, even if left out.
Expressing, when in doubt.
Moves with heart and
shows off the skills of brain.
Expert in nothing
but experienced in everything.

The 'unknown' in my house.

Left, when the door was closed,
but tried a lot to get along.
I took a safer hand to leave
to lead me in light
while the 'unknown' thought –
darkness was necessary
for me to shine.

NOTHING WILL BREAK YOUR FLIGHT

Lose your backpack,
untie the knots,
relax a while,
think not.

Turn the eyes
towards positives
and let all negativity flow.

Disobey your reasonable thoughts
and break free
towards the sky
you desired with a hope.

You got wings,
not to shut it down.
Flying is your passion,
don't let darkness
bring you down.

You are not a hero in disguise,
you are just a person
trying hard
to fix some lives.

Believe in yourself,
because that's how
you would smile.
And then nothing
in this world
will ever break
your flight.

YOU!

It's not wrong,
if for once in a while
your heart calls out
for just you!

You think,
they will call you selfish
but it's okay to be
what's true.

They will call you names
even though you decide
to take theirs loads
on your shoulder.

Easy going!
they would gossip about you.
So why not be a
hard ass for once.

It's okay if they are not happy.
What really matters
in the end is you!
I agree it's not always

about you!
But sometimes it's okay
to disagree
and try something new.

IT'S OKAY!

I ran a race
and ended up
in second place.

I saw the faces,
the ones who said they loved me.
They all looked
disappointed today.

Their smiles were fake,
and their claps had no echo.
I kept searching for appreciation,
but all I got is - *it's okay*!

It's okay! A new way to say,
it's not okay.
A way to tell you,
that it's bad to lose.

Maybe it is,
but not the winners
have a chance to prove,
it's the looser
who gets the chance to win new!

Well, I took that *it's okay*
and used it in a different way.

It's okay,
if I have lost…it was me performing,
not you!
It's okay,
if I slipped…it was me running,
not you!

Why give yourself a hard time,
if in your head you know
you will work on it again.
It's okay to be a looser,
for a looser would know
what it really means to win!

TO BE WITH MY SELF

I walked with myself at 2 am
Trust me, it was romantic,
I was the one talking,
and I was the one keenly
listening to each word I said.

I even made myself smile,
that wasn't as hard as I'd thought.
I watched my back,
I held myself up,
I thought of crying at some points,
but I was there for me,
to wipe my tears.

I felt new,
how surprising it was
to get to know the real me.
Ever I was interested
in what I really loved?
Was it really hard,
to care about my hands,
not banging them
on the walls in anger?

In the process of
finding the world,
looking out for them who thought
it was easier to let me go.
I somehow had forgotten
how it really felt
to be with my self.

THE WAY I WALKED!

Right foot first
and then the next one,
I walked like this all my life.
A pattern my father taught me
when I was a child.

One day, I came home
with a crooked walk,
my feet couldn't
hold my weight anymore.

It was hurting,
not bleeding but had an
internal wound.
So, I changed my walk
to manage to move.

I expected a hand for support,
but instead I got a look!
A look that said it all,
I broke the pattern,
it was not how I was
supposed to walk.

How did I go so wrong?
I was an innocent child once.
What got into my head?
was I turning into a vagabond?

They judged me
all they could,
and all this happened
because I changed
the way I walked!

INCOMPLETE JOURNEY

A lot of roads are
yet to be travelled
Don't give up
on the first road.

I know it was hard,
to walk on that path
leading you nowhere.

Well, it brought you here!
Here you are!
Stronger than ever,
wiser than the people
you left behind.

Look at your scars,
they make you who you are.
They shine like the gold
used to fix the pot.

Still a long journey
is ahead of you.
You might again fall,
loose or maybe it will all work out.

But you don't know that yet,
all you got is a hope in your heart.
Take that hope and trust it.

Even though you might envy
the ones who got it all
but trust me no one has
completed their journey.

It broke me
because I was eager.

It hurt me
because I was vulnerable.

It angered me
because I was immature.

It stopped me from smiling
Because I kept pinching
my arms.

It burned me
because it was all
that I thought.

I couldn't find my spirit,
it wasn't lost.
I'd covered it
with the scars.

What was to blame –
my ego, my anxiety,

my insecurity
or the love
that was suppose
to console.

CHANGING ME

Nerdy me,
or judgy you?
Selfish me,
or self-centered you?

Crazy me,
or stickler you?
Laid back me,
or uptight you?

Calm me,
or anxious you?
Looser me,
or safer you?

Dancing me,
or watching you?
Living my life even though one day
I would be blue.
Changing me,
or constant you?

DEADLINE

November noon.
Sitting on a bench,
analyzing the day
for how to spend.

It had been six weeks,
today I had left my bed.
My thighs still aching,
my neck – hard to move.
My eyes burning
due to all the movies I watched
in my phone.

I made seven friends online
and talked to each of them
at their suitable time.
Three of them were girls,
and rest were boys.
I told no one, how injured I was.
Sympathy was off the table
to deal with for my mind.

The pills I popped – tasted good, day by day.
The water turned colored for me,

and liquid was my food
for they said I couldn't chew
due to my broken jaw.

Life had stopped,
I was on an unplanned vacation.
The last day of my job,
when I remember had three deadlines
All the dependencies were on me.
They said, it won't work,
If I didn't work an extra shift.

I had woken up early,
sat with my computer,
staring hard on the screen.
Thinking of the meetings to attend
and the answers to give.
I hopped in my car early that day,
the road was empty,
so smooth was my ride.

My phone rang,
it was my colleague,
it went straight between my neck
and ears and 'hello' was all I'd said.
My phone slipped from my shoulders
and I was afraid it would break,

totally forgetting it would fall
on the leather seat.
In a sudden reaction, I moved to save it.
The steering turned wrong,
the car hit the divider
and I could see myself flying
with my turning car.

I was admitted while I was unconscious.
Five days later when I woke up,
I was unmovable.
I would lie on the bed
and just turn my eyes,
closing them every now and then.
I thought about the deadlines,
which I had left.
But there was no way for me
to know the status.

Today, November noon.
Sitting on a bench,
analyzing the day
for how to spend.

I spoke to my colleague in the morning
to ask about what had happened
with the deadline six months back.

He told it was past
and pushed for a new date and time.
Apparently, the company had got an excuse
to present in front of the client.
Soon after that, they replaced me
with a temporary resource
who was able to complete the work,
before the extended deadline.

TRAP OF PARADOX

I knew I was broke,
When the fingers pointing at me,
were my own.

It was a trap of paradox.
My conscience was disagreeing
with its own reason.

I was wrong,
and all that was wrong happened
because of my treason.

I'd betrayed the right,
defined by me.
It felt like a hole,
pierced through my ribs.

And the blood from my heart
was leaking through my eyes.
A second of silence
was tough to find.
I had stopped the flow,
the flow of love.

Towards myself, apparently
that was what mattered.
To fix the hole,
to cut the trap,
it was necessary for me
to look at myself from the eyes,
not my own.

WHO AM I?

Who am I?
the person,
flesh and bone,
the dream,
or a just an illusion?

I follow the tracks,
set by the world
Who made that right?
Was it always this way?
or there was a revolution?
Why do I feel that my hands are tied?

Why is it a crime,
to walk a path
which is self-defined?
What's the matter with
the world?
Why am I being ruled
by a certain people?
Is there really a freedom
or just an illusion?

Who am I?
the mirror of someone,
a moral, a lesson
or just a user of time?

I follow the clock,
I follow the orders,
I follow the nuisance
Why do I do, what I do?
Am I really supposed to?

Why can't I just rule myself?
Why am I not the owner
 of my decisions?
Why do I have to feel helpless
most of the time?
Why can't I lose myself
in something that I love?

NOT YOU!

A drama, you are?
So be it.
Nobody else can
be that for you.

Talk like an idiot,
if they say so.
Nobody else can
speak for you.

Your thoughts are cliché?
Share it.
There are people
who don't know about it yet

Don't try to be
somebody else,
Because somebody else
is not you!

DREAMT OF

Come on, once again,
let's try hard to live like
what we dreamt of.

Pick yourself up,
decorate your scars,
make your steps count,
that's how loud
the noise should be.

You are here,
because you deserve the space,
the air, the truth and
the beauty
the world beholds.

Come on, once again,
let's try hard to live like
what we dreamt of.

I broke that chain,
and all the attachments.

Stood up and
wore my breast plate,
powdered my cheek,
rubbed my lips
with a dark lipstick.

Turned around to
check my back,
it looked perfect
and I am proud of that.

The nails were done,
eye lashes brushed,
my hairs hanged
over my shoulder
and I felt like an angel.

The chin should be up,
I told myself.
Eyes should look
directly at the world,

I am beautiful and
I don't need
a compliment.

WHAT YOU WISH!

The devil hears you,
Waiting to grant
the dark wishes.

You speak the ill
about yourself,
your wish is granted.

So, watch out,
don't speak foul
of yourself.
Let the devil think,
there is nothing darker in you.

LEARN TO LAUGH

Sitting in your class,
if they tease you hard.
Learn to laugh.

Walking down, a lonely path,
if they call out names,
learn to laugh.

Wear your smile
as a jewel of gold.
It makes you calm,
as if nothing in this world
can break your heart.

Why to show,
you are vulnerable?
For maybe they would use
it as a weapon
to destroy your soul.

Blaming they are, on you
to drop you into guilt.
Learn to laugh.

Laugh on yourself,
for it will take of the weight
of embarrassment
and maybe put it on the shoulders
of the people who were
calling out your name.

DON'T LET THEM

Don't let them
fool you,
You are too good to be
the mediocre.

They would ask you
to settle
for it's the best choice,
You don't allow
your dreams to settle down.

Don't let them
make you doubt
on your abilities,
You have something,
they surely don't have.

Don't let them
guide you,
If they don't know
how it feels to walk on
the hard path.

They would ask you

to take it easy,
You don't allow yourself
to relax until you have reached
where you are meant to be.

Don't let them
fill your mind
with materialistic desires,
You have to keep your heart
focused like a rising star.

Let them talk,
let them doubt,
let them laugh,
let them speak the false
and let them believe they are true.

Only if they would have
had the guts
to face the world,
they wouldn't have so much energy
left to judge you.

UP THERE

If you think following rules
is stopping you,
to move forward.
Break that god damn rule.

Because no one cares how you
reached at the top,
they just get inspired
or jealous by seeing you
up there.

CRAZY... CREATES...

The open eyes
born from which
is a dream I see
and live each day.

The mind takes
all its efforts to get distracted
but the heart
keeps me in a direction
where none matters but
the dream of the open eyes.

My habits
will slowly change,
My behaviour
will be altered,
I could stop
acting normal.
Turning introvert
maybe only the option left.

My eyes will be
opened all the time,
Sleep will

become a liability.

They would say,
I will go crazy,
but I know,
crazy.... creates...

TOXIC

If you wish to change things.
Close your mind for toxic elements around you.

Let them be the people,
or be the situation.

Let them claim,
they love you a lot!
when all they want is attention.

Don't let them feed
on your peace of mind, for it's rare.

Let them talk
and let them laugh
and let them be where they are.
Don't invite.

Keep a smile on your face
and don't give a damn...

LETS

Let's rise today
and grow into unexpected.

Let's change that one habit,
that made us feel rejected.
Rejected by our own vision,
our own true self.

Let's change for ourselves,
let's collect all our broken pieces
and put them together.

Let's try to love
the imperfect us.
Let's be
unapologetically us.

ABUNDANCE IN ME

There is a music in me.
There is an art in me.
There is a creativity
which I couldn't see.

There are some words in me,
ready to be written.
There is a story in me,
waiting to be told.

There is an idea,
I have been waiting to execute.
There is an abundance in me,
ready to be shared with the world.

A BLANK CANVAS

A blank canvas,
about to paint.
The first stroke
of color red.
Painted a heart,
broken on the edges.

Cleaned the area
for people to fit in.
Dropped a few names,
can't say!
The rest were
allowed to take a place,
happy indeed was
my painting ahead.

More and more
people popped,
I knew they all
needed a place.
Some with love,
some showing pain,
some wanted it
because they thought

they were deserving of the space.

The canvas
got crowded,
even the heart
didn't look the same.

Something had to be done,
so took a black paint
and throwed all over the page.
Everything was
covered in black
but now the canvas
had a lot of space.

Again, a stroke of red was made,
a heart was painted
but this time
only the ones
I wanted got the place.

GROWING YOUR WINGS

How far I would go?
It would be a tragic road.

But wait a second,
did I ever pray
for an easier journey?

What I wished was
at the other side
of the turmoil.

So, what's about all this
complains and blaming?
I wanted to fly –
So, I must undergo the pain
of growing wings.

It would not pop out from nowhere.
It would grow out by tearing
my muscles and
breaking my bones.

The process would be slow
and full of pain.

But once it's out,
a flap would be enough.

Enough to initially hover over
the land and later fly right there,
up in the sky,
looking down and watching
your perseverance
that would make
everything smaller.

OUR HEART TELLS...

I find it amazing,
how beautiful - mind thinks.
It's like a box full of spells,
we need to learn,
how the wand swings.

Innovation, development,
creativity is born there.
It has the capacity
to change the world –
with just a dream.

But our mind has legs
and it runs.
Actually, it has many legs,
all running in many directions.

One who can control it
is considered as a *yogi*,
while the one who is controlled by it
is considered as a *bhogi*.

Mind craves for attention,
hence proposing weird activities.

Some for pleasure,
some for pain,
while others are just
the catalyst
for the completely new game.

We need to train
our self to choose,
choose the words spoken
by the mind
and how it is going to affect us.

It may take
our sanity, our reasoning,
and our spine.
Broken are the people
who surrender,
to the willingness of the mind.

It's not a villain,
just impressionable.
Follows the misery
if addicted
and loses itself
if irrational.

Try hard to control,

it will turn you
into mess.
The only option is
to focus
on what really
our heart tells.

RIGHT NOW, IS LIFE

Ever found yourself
craving for something new.
Usually when you realize,
between all the chaos,
your words are respected
only by few.

There is a voice inside –
screaming, complaining
and asking for rescue.

Ever found yourself
walking too slow
and realizing something
is not right?

Do you also remember,
the motivation
which put you
to sleep last night –
You trusted
your journey
and decided to give a fight.

But are you still,
not started
or are you waiting
for the situation
to be alright?

What stops us to act?
Is it your nature,
to plan and not start?
Because if you are
not for yourself
who is for you?

Remember,
life is a long journey
and excuses
would be a nasty ride.

Take out your wings
that you are hiding
and explore your real side.

You are meant to fly
to your dreams
and not to hide.

Do yourself a favour

and don't look behind,
because what's gone
is a history
and what's ahead
is a mystery
and what's right now
 is LIFE.

TALK TO YOURSELF

Talk to yourself.
Talk positive,
repeat the good words.
Make sure you remember –
That how precious are you.

I know there have been
hard times, bad experiences.
But you are still here,
make it count.
There is nothing important then you.
The world can be searched for,
but you can't find
anyone else like you.

Talk to yourself.
But don't over analyse.
It's alright if you have
a different definition for everything
that's been believed otherwise.
Your words should be
first respected by you.
Before you find people, who would
agree with you.

Talk to yourself about
who you want to become?
Give yourself a plan
but not an ultimatum.
The duration of life is unexpected
but still hope is what you should favour.

The light at the end of the tunnel
is what we all work for.
Don't let yourself back out.
Take a step forward.
And still if you can't trust.
Talk to yourself.
Talk positive
and repeat the good words.

ABOUT THE AUTHOR

Raviraj Mishra, born in Pune, India is a writer and an
entrepreneur. He is the author of the book - The Feeling of
Being Loved. He started writing when he was 12 years of
age and soon he developed a habit of reading stories and
creating one for himself.

He started blogging from 2014. His blog mostly consisted
of short stories or dramatic scenes. He wrote more than 50
short stories and poems before he started working on his
first book - The Feeling of Being Loved.

Being a newbie in the publishing world he decided to
publish a short book of his 11 selected stories for an

experience. The book was called '11 Stories - Stories of Love, Life and Everything'. It was published in June 2019 and after 5 months, he published his first full novel "The Feeling of Being Loved"

The Book is available across the world through some major sellers like Amazon, Flipkart, Kindle, smashwords and Google books.

Website: www.ravirajmishra.com

Instagram : www.instagram.com/imravirajmishra/

www.ingramcontent.com/pod-product-compliance
Lightning Source LLC
Chambersburg PA
CBHW051006060726

47593CB00017B/1098